Food As Fuel:
Nutrition fo
Athletes

KRISTIN PETRIE MS, RD
ABDO Publishing Company

visit us at
www.abdopublishing.com

Published by ABDO Publishing Company, 8000 West 78th Street, Edina, Minnesota 55439.
Copyright © 2012 by Abdo Consulting Group, Inc. International copyrights reserved in all
countries. No part of this book may be reproduced in any form without written permission from the
publisher. The Checkerboard Library™ is a trademark and logo of ABDO Publishing Company.

Printed in the United States of America, North Mankato, Minnesota.
062011
092011

 PRINTED ON RECYCLED PAPER

Cover Photos: Photolibrary, iStockphoto
Interior Photos: AP Images p. 15; Corbis pp. 25, 29; Getty Images pp. 5, 6, 7, 9, 11, 12, 14, 17, 19,
    20, 27; Glow Images p. 13; iStockphoto pp. 1, 23; Photo Researchers p. 26

Series Coordinator: BreAnn Rumsch
Editors: Megan M. Gunderson, BreAnn Rumsch
Art Direction: Neil Klinepier

Library of Congress Cataloging-in-Publication Data

Petrie, Kristin, 1970-
  Food as fuel : nutrition for athletes / Kristin Petrie.
      p. cm. -- (Mission: Nutrition)
  Includes index.
  ISBN 978-1-61783-081-5
  1. Athletes--Nutrition--Juvenile literature. 2. Sports--Physiological aspects--Juvenile literature. 3.
Exercise--Physiological aspects--Juvenile literature. I. Title.
  TX361.A8P467 2012
  613.2024796--dc22
                            2011010389

Contents

Feed Your Body

Are you a spirited sports fan? Do you also love being active? If you regularly participate in a sport, you're an athlete.

Every athlete knows the importance of practice and training. Runners push themselves on the track so they're first across the finish line. Divers leap again and again to perfect their form.

Practice and training help athletes prepare their minds and bodies for physical activity. Many people rely on these alone to succeed in their sport or activity. But this is a mistake!

Smart athletes know that proper **nutrition** is an equally important part of their success. It helps refuel the energy their bodies use during physical activity. Eating right also helps prevent injury and aids recovery.

Athletes are more likely to perform their best when they eat the right foods. So keep reading to learn how to fuel your own performance!

Proper nutrition is the foundation of success for any athlete.

The Right Stuff

Balance, variety, and moderation are the goals of a healthy diet. This is true for all athletes, young or old. But, do you really know what a balanced diet is?

It means eating some, but not too much, from all five food groups. These are grains, fruits, vegetables, dairy, and protein. Fats and sugars are not a food group, but they are another necessary part of your diet. Eating a wide variety of foods helps meet your body's **calorie** and **nutrient** needs.

It may help you to picture this balanced diet as a plate of food. The plate has one **serving** of vegetables and another of fruit. Brightly colored fruits and vegetables are

Vary your vegetables. They have much to offer your body!

Fruits are a tasty treat as well as good for you!

rich in vitamins and minerals. So oranges, strawberries, squash, and corn are great choices.

If you want to react quickly or have good aim, eat your fruits and veggies! Minerals such as magnesium and potassium are needed for energy and growth. They also help your muscles move and your **organs** operate. Vitamins such as A and C do a lot, too! They keep your eyes and skin healthy and strengthen your bones.

Now keep picturing that balanced plate of food. It also has some lean meat, fish, eggs, or other protein. Most kids know that protein builds strong muscles. Did you know it also helps build your bones, **tendons**, and skin? Your muscles wouldn't get you very far without those!

A **serving** from the grains group also takes up space on the plate. Pasta, bread, rice, and other high-**carbohydrate** foods provide lots of energy. But not all grains are the same!

Whole grains don't have their outer layer stripped away. This layer holds most of the grain's **fiber**, vitamins, and protein. So, whole wheat bread and brown rice will provide lots of **nutrients**. White bread and white rice provide less because they are not whole grains.

A serving from the dairy group rounds off the plate. A cup of yogurt or a slice of cheese on your burger are good examples. Foods from this group provide calcium and protein for your growing bones. They are also great sources of some of the B vitamins. These vitamins help your body turn the foods you eat into fuel.

Last but not least, a balanced diet includes some fats and sugars. Your body performs best on healthy fats, such as those in olives and nuts. Less healthy fats come from meat, dairy, and fried foods. You already know what foods have sugar. Sweets!

What is the key to a successful balanced diet? Eat a variety of foods in moderation. And feed your body the **nutrients** it needs first. Then you can see if there's room for dessert!

Calcium will protect your bones to keep you in the game!

How Much?

More, more, more! Yes, young athletes usually need to eat more than less active kids. What and how much to eat are important decisions. These choices can affect your health and performance.

So, how much more? The amount of food a young athlete needs depends on a couple of factors. First, how much energy is being used? Daily basketball practice will burn more **calories** than an occasional game of hoops.

A less obvious factor is the rate at which you are growing. At your age, you might be growing super fast! But the amount of growth can change from day to day and week to week. Luckily, your body will tell you when it needs more fuel. Some basic signals are a growling stomach, low energy, or weight loss.

Sometimes your body will order, "Eat more!" Does this mean you should go crazy and eat lots of junk food? No way! Kids in sports need to select good foods that make them stronger and healthier. The right foods provide extra energy, increased bone strength, and faster recovery after exercise.

Food provides your body with the energy it needs for your active lifestyle.

The Big Three

Whatever your sport, you need to eat **carbohydrates**, protein, and fat for energy. You start **digesting** these **nutrients** in your mouth and stomach. They finish breaking down in your intestines. There, your body absorbs them.

Carbs are your biggest source of fuel. Simple carbohydrates come from sweets, fruits, and sports drinks. Your body breaks them down fast. So, they quickly deliver small amounts of energy.

Whole grains in bread and pasta deliver complex

Glycogen stores in your body are the fuel behind your performance on the field.

carbohydrates. These take longer to break down. So, they provide energy at a slower pace. This energy also lasts longer.

After you eat, your body breaks down carbohydrates into **glucose**, which enters your blood. Your blood carries some to areas of your body that need energy right away. This might be your muscles or brain.

When the glucose arrives, it is turned into energy. Other glucose is stored in the muscles and liver as glycogen.

Foods with protein help tired muscles recover and grow stronger.

Glycogen is the main source of fuel your body uses. It provides bursts of energy for short-term activities such as running sprints. It also fuels activities that last longer, such as swimming.

Protein is another necessary part of your diet. It doesn't store well in your body. So, it must be replaced often by what you eat. Athletic activities demand a lot of energy from your muscles! They need protein to repair and rebuild themselves.

Fat often gets a bad rap. Yet it is important for athletes in many ways. Fat absorbs and stores certain vitamins. These include A, E, and K. Vitamin A helps you see the ball. Vitamin E helps your sore muscles heal. Vitamin K keeps you from bleeding too much when you get hurt.

A sandwich with meat, veggies, and cheese is a well-balanced meal to fuel your body's needs.

Fat also produces tons of energy. Energy from fat is key during long activities when energy from other sources runs out. However, getting energy from fat is hard work. Your body has to burn up extra oxygen to turn fat into fuel.

Like too much of anything, too much fat can be harmful. It can affect your health and how you perform. But everyone needs some body fat! It acts like a pillow that protects your **organs**.

An athlete should not rely on protein or fat for energy. Why? Protein's first job is to build muscles! In addition, turning protein or fat into energy is hard work. The energy used to do this would be better spent on your activity! So, eating **carbohydrates** is the easiest way to fuel up.

Body Boost

Certain minerals are a must for athletes. For example, calcium is critical for bone growth and strength. An athlete's bones take a beating from running, jumping, and **colliding**. Calcium builds **dense**, strong bones. Strong bones are less likely to break during sports activities.

Calcium is also important for muscle control. Want to kick a ball or throw a pitch? Every muscle you use needs calcium to work effectively. Three to four **servings** of dairy foods per day will help you get enough.

Iron is another mineral of great importance for athletes. It is found in hemoglobin, which carries oxygen in your blood. Every cell in your body requires oxygen to work. Without enough iron, you feel tired and weak. That won't help you on the field!

Luckily, iron isn't hard to find. Red meats are a rich source. Fortified foods, such as breakfast cereals and breads, are also a good source. These foods have had iron added to them.

Getting enough calcium and iron in your diet will help you compete!

Chug, Chug!

Water, water, water! Why is everyone telling you to drink so much water? Water plays as important a role in sports **nutrition** as food does.

Without enough water, your body cannot make use of the food you eat. Water helps your body break down your food. It also helps your blood move the **nutrients** from food around your body. In addition, water keeps your joints **lubricated** and your tissues and **organs** padded. These are extremely important jobs!

However, water has yet another important job to do. It regulates your body temperature. When your muscles work hard, they create lots of heat. Your body releases heat through sweat, or water. Sweat on your skin **evaporates**. This has a cooling effect.

Cooling is necessary, but it can cause very large losses of water. When lost water is not replaced, you become dehydrated. This may not seem like a big deal. But it affects many key body parts. Without enough water, your body simply cannot function.

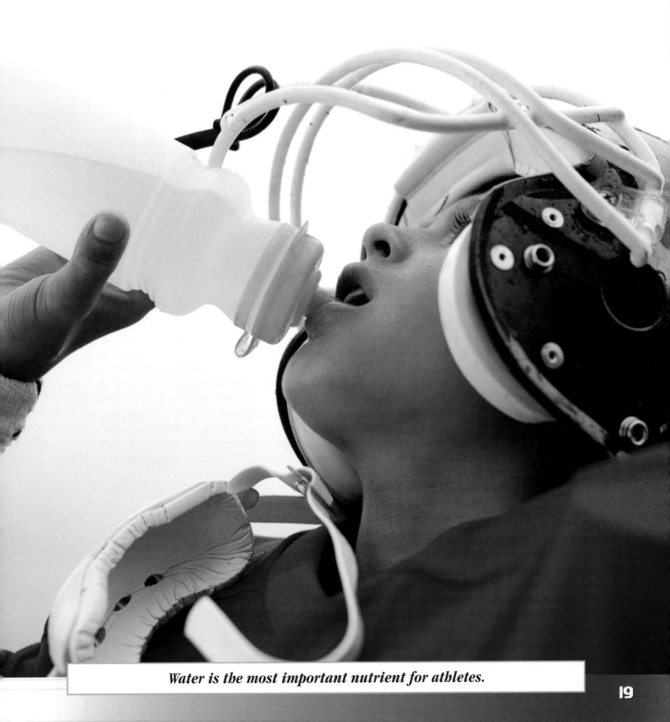

Water is the most important nutrient for athletes.

Did you know that more than 80% of your blood is water? So when you are dehydrated, there is less blood to flow in your veins. This causes your heart to work harder to keep blood moving around your body. Less blood flow also means less oxygen delivered to your brain.

How much water do you need? There is no one easy answer. Everyone needs different amounts, and it depends on many factors. These include how long and demanding your activity is. The rate at which you sweat is also important. The temperature and altitude of your surroundings matter, too.

To be well hydrated, drink water throughout the day, especially when you are thirsty. On game day, drink fluids before, during, and after your event. You may not feel thirsty, and you may not be sweating. However, your young body needs to be well hydrated to perform its many jobs.

What's a simple way to tell if you're getting enough water? Look at the color of your urine. Light yellow urine is a good sign. Dark yellow urine that looks like apple juice usually signals you need more water. If you are confused or concerned about your hydration, ask an adult for help.

Danger Decoder

Dehydration can sneak up on you. Even mild dehydration can start a long list of problems. So do your best to get enough fluids. But also be aware of signs of trouble. Early signs include thirst and sweating. Next, muscles may cramp and feel tired or weak. Dizziness and confusion mean serious trouble.

Power Up

When it is time for the big game, you want to be ready. Most of the fuel used during sports activities is from glycogen. Remember, this is the **glucose** your body has stored from your regular diet. So what you eat between games, meets, and matches is important!

Eating the right kind of food at the right time affects your ability to get in the game. Eating too close to your event can make you feel uncomfortable or sick. And, your body will use some energy for **digestion**. That energy cannot help fuel your activity.

Your pregame meal is an important one. It should resemble a regular meal. Eat a slightly larger portion of **carbohydrates**, such as pasta. Include a **serving** of skim milk, chicken, or another low-fat, high-protein food. Choose fruits and vegetables low in **fiber**, such as melon and carrots. These round off your meal without leading to slow digestion.

About one hour before your activity, you should eat a light snack. It should be high in carbs, low in fat, and moderate in fiber. Yogurt, fruit, and dried cereal are good choices. Energy bars may seem like convenient snacks. But some energy bars have ingredients you don't want. Simple sugars, fat, and too much protein can actually limit your performance.

Chew On This

Carbohydrate loading is a practice that many athletes talk about. Unlike people often believe, it does not mean eating as many carbs as possible before an event. Rather, it is a training method for adult athletes. They change their eating and exercise habits over a period of time. This is done to store as much glycogen as possible. Carbohydrate loading is not necessary or effective for kids in sports.

Refueling

Congratulations! You crossed the finish line. You finished your game. You gave it your all! And your great eating habits gave you lots of energy. Now it's time to replace what you used.

The first thing to do after your activity is to rehydrate. Drinking water to satisfy your thirst is a good start. Then drink some more!

Sports drinks made with simple **carbohydrates** and **electrolytes** are also available. But ask a parent or coach for guidance. In general, water or fruit juices should meet your needs.

The next step is to refuel. Should you fill up on pizza, chips, and ice cream? No, those are probably not the best choices. Instead, choose a good source of carbs. Eat within 30 minutes to help replace glycogen in your muscles. Help replace it more **efficiently** by adding protein. Your snack can be as simple as a bagel with turkey slices.

Proper rehydration and refueling improve your body's recovery and reduce your risk of injury. They also set you up for continued training and great performance.

Replace lost fluids as soon as possible after finishing your activity. You'll feel better the rest of the day!

Your Safe Diet

You now know how to fuel for exercise. Don't forget that your body has its own needs! This means that another athlete's balanced plate may not look like yours.

For example, vegetarians do not eat meat. They must take special care to get enough calcium, iron, zinc, vitamin B_{12}, and protein. That's because these usually come from animal-based foods. Careful planning is needed to create a balanced diet for a young vegetarian athlete.

Does your sport place importance on your body weight and size? Young athletes often

A nutrition expert can show you how to eat right for your body's needs.

Paying attention to your body's needs means you'll be in the best shape for you!

feel pressure to follow weight-loss diets. They may decide on their own to diet. Or, they start because someone told them to. Unfortunately, these diets rarely meet the needs of a young person's growing body. In addition, dieting can lead to **eating disorders**.

The bottom line is that young people, especially athletes, shouldn't diet. Are you worried about your weight? Has someone suggested you lose weight? If so, talk to a trusted adult. Your growing, active body is very special. You need to treat it well so it performs at its best!

A Healthier You

Are you an athlete who wants to play longer, faster, or harder? Or maybe you haven't played a sport before but feel ready to give it a try. With proper nutrition, you'll be on the right track to meet your goal! Check out these tips from the *Let's Move!* program. They will help you develop a more active lifestyle.

GET OFF THE COUCH! There are lots of ways to entertain yourself without electronic devices. Replace some of that screen time with time outdoors. Run, bike, hike, or explore!

JOIN THE COMMUNITY! Many towns have parks, playgrounds, and community centers. See if one near you offers classes. You could take up dance, gymnastics, swimming, or a team sport.

Let's Move!

For more information, check out *Let's Move!* online at **www.letsmove.gov**.

Let's Move! is a campaign started by First Lady Michelle Obama to raise a healthier generation of kids and combat childhood obesity. This movement works to provide schools, families, and communities with the tools to help kids be more active, eat better, and live healthfully.

The *Let's Move!* Web site provides information about the movement. It includes recipes as well as helpful tips on nutrition and physical activity. And, there are action tools to promote healthier foods in your local schools or start a *Let's Move!* Meetup.

REST UP! Just like running around, a good night's sleep is key to your health. Most kids ages 5 to 10 need ten hours each night. Kids over age 10 need nine hours each night.

GET REWARDED! Take part in physical activity five days a week for six weeks. This commitment can earn you the Presidential Active Lifestyle Award!

Glossary

calorie - the unit of measure for the energy supplied by food.

carbohydrate (cahr-boh-HEYE-drayt) - a substance made by plants, which serves as a major class of foods for animals. Sugar and starch are examples of carbohydrates.

collide - to come together with force.

dense - having a high mass per unit volume.

digest - to break down food into simpler substances the body can absorb. Digestion is the process of digesting.

eating disorder - any of several mental conditions marked by serious changes in eating behavior.

efficient - wasting little time or energy.

electrolyte (ih-LEHK-truh-lite) - a substance that regulates or affects certain processes in the body.

evaporate - to change from a liquid or a solid into a vapor.

fiber - a material found in edible plants that normally passes undigested through the body. It promotes the healthy functioning of the stomach and intestines.

glucose - a naturally occurring form of sugar found in plants, fruits, and blood. It is a source of energy for living things.

lubricate - to make smooth or slippery.

nutrient - a substance found in food and used in the body. It promotes growth, maintenance, and repair.

nutrition - that which promotes growth, provides energy, repairs body tissues, and maintains life. Nutrition is also the study of nutrients and the processes of using, storing, and eliminating these substances.

organ - a part of an animal or a plant composed of several kinds of tissues. An organ performs a specific function. Organs of an animal include the heart, the brain, and the eyes.

serving - a unit of measure used to describe the recommended amount of a food or drink.

tendon - a band of tough fibers that joins a muscle to another body part, such as a bone.

Web Sites

To learn more about nutrition for athletes, visit ABDO Publishing Company online. Web sites about using food as fuel are featured on our Book Links page. These links are routinely monitored and updated to provide the most current information available.

www.abdopublishing.com

Index

A
activity 4, 10, 14, 15, 16, 18, 21, 22, 24, 26

B
balanced diet 6, 8, 9, 22, 26
blood 13, 16, 18, 21
bones 8, 10, 16

C
calories 6, 10
carbohydrates 8, 12, 13, 15, 22, 24

D
dairy 6, 8, 9, 16, 22
dehydration 18, 21
dieting 27
digestion 12, 13, 18, 22

E
eating disorders 27
electrolytes 24
energy 4, 8, 10, 12, 13, 14, 15, 22, 24

F
fats 6, 9, 12, 14, 15, 22, 23
fiber 8, 22
food groups 6, 8, 9, 12, 14, 15, 16, 22, 23, 24, 26
fruits 6, 8, 12, 22, 24

G
glucose 13, 22
glycogen 13, 14, 22, 24
grains 6, 8, 12, 16, 22, 24
growth 8, 10, 16, 27

H
health 4, 6, 8, 10, 15, 18, 21, 22, 27

I
injury 4, 14, 16, 24

M
minerals 8, 16, 26
muscles 8, 13, 14, 15, 16, 18, 24

O
organs 8, 10, 12, 13, 15, 18, 21

P
performance 4, 8, 9, 10, 14, 15, 16, 18, 21, 22, 23, 24, 27
protein 6, 8, 9, 12, 14, 15, 16, 22, 23, 24, 26

R
recovery 4, 10, 14, 24

S
sugars 6, 9, 12, 23

T
training 4, 24

V
vegetables 6, 8, 22
vegetarians 26
vitamins 8, 14, 26

W
water 18, 21, 24
weight 10, 26, 27